Infinite Reflections

Recognizing Patterns, Healing from the Past, and Creating the True You.

Copyright Notice

Disclaimer

The information provided in this book, "Infinite Reflections: Recognizing Patterns, Healing from the Past, and Creating the True You," is intended for general informational purposes only. While every effort has been made to ensure the accuracy and completeness of the information presented, the author and publisher assume no responsibility for errors or omissions, or for any results obtained from the use of the information contained in this book. Readers are encouraged to exercise their own judgment and seek professional advice if needed.

Contents

Introduction

In the intricate tapestry of human existence, each life is woven with a myriad of experiences, emotions, and relationships. Our journey is marked by the interplay of joy and sorrow, success and failure, love and heartbreak. Yet, within this complex mosaic, certain patterns emerge—patterns that reflect not only the external circumstances but also the internal landscape of our minds and hearts.

"Infinite Reflections: Recognizing Patterns, Healing from the Past, and Creating the True You" invites you on a profound exploration of these patterns, offering a transformative guide to understanding, healing, and embracing the essence of your true self.

Life unfolds in patterns that repeat, both seen and unseen, manifesting in our thoughts, behaviors, and relationships. The echoes of our past experiences, both delightful and painful, resonate through time, shaping our perceptions and influencing our choices. This book delves into the patterns that often go unnoticed, providing insightful perspectives and practical tools to unravel the threads of the past.

As we become attuned to the intricate rhythms of our lives, we gain the power to break free from limiting cycles and chart a course toward authentic self-discovery.

"Infinite Reflections" serves as a beacon of self-awareness, guiding readers on a journey of introspection and empowerment. This book illuminates the path to healing and self-realization. It encourages readers to embrace the totality of their experiences, recognizing that every reflection, no matter how distorted, holds the potential for growth and renewal.

The journey toward the true self is not linear, nor is it without challenges. However, by understanding the patterns that govern our lives, we gain the wisdom to navigate the twists and turns with resilience and grace. This book is an invitation to embark on a profound inner quest—one that leads to the core of your being, where authenticity, purpose, and fulfillment await.

As you turn the pages of "Infinite Reflections," may you find the inspiration to embark on a transformative odyssey—one that brings clarity to the past, illuminates the present, and unveils the boundless potential of the future. The mirror of self-discovery awaits, reflecting the infinite possibilities that emerge when you recognize the patterns, heal from the past, and create the true you.

Chapter 1

Unveiling Your Patterns

Patterns are an inherent part of the human experience, influencing our thoughts, behaviors, and ultimately shaping the course of our lives. Unveiling these patterns is a crucial step towards self-awareness and personal growth. In this chapter, we will explore the profound impact of patterns on our lives, delve into the intricacies of understanding their influence, and discuss strategies for identifying repetitive behaviors and thoughts.

Understanding the Influence of Patterns in Your Life

The Subconscious Blueprint

The concept of the subconscious blueprint encapsulates the intricate web of beliefs, attitudes, and automatic responses that shape an individual's perception of themselves and the world. Rooted in early life experiences, cultural influences, and societal norms, the subconscious blueprint operates beneath the surface of conscious awareness, yet profoundly guides behavior, emotions, and decision-making.

This neural framework, etched through a lifetime of interactions and internalizations, forms the lens through which individuals interpret their surroundings and navigate their lives. Understanding the subconscious blueprint provides a gateway to self-awareness, offering insights into the origins of habits, emotional patterns, and self-perceptions, ultimately empowering individuals to consciously shape and evolve their mental frameworks for a more fulfilling and intentional life.

Influence on Behavior

The subconscious blueprint plays a pivotal role in guiding automatic responses to stimuli, a phenomenon that shapes a significant portion of human behavior without conscious intent.

Deeply rooted in the neural networks of the

brain, the subconscious blueprint is the repository of learned associations, experiences, and responses.

The process of automatic response begins with the encoding of experiences into the subconscious. Through repetition and reinforcement, behaviors, emotions, and thoughts become ingrained in the subconscious blueprint. This encoding is particularly salient for emotionally charged experiences, as the amygdala, a key component of the limbic system, is highly involved in the storage and retrieval of emotional memories.

When stimuli are encountered, the subconscious blueprint swiftly retrieves relevant information to generate an automatic response. This process is akin to a mental shortcut, allowing for rapid decision-making without the need for conscious deliberation. For example, if an individual has experienced trauma associated with a particular sound, the subconscious may trigger an automatic fear response upon hearing that sound in the future.

The automatic responses guided by the subconscious blueprint are not limited to external stimuli. Internal cues, such as thoughts and emotions, also trigger automatic reactions. For instance, negative self-talk stemming from deep-seated beliefs stored in the subconscious can automatically evoke feelings of self-doubt and anxiety.

Limiting Beliefs and Self-Sabotage

The subconscious blueprint serves as a repository for belief systems that wield profound influence over how individuals perceive themselves and the world around them. Shaped by a culmination of experiences, societal influences, and early-life conditioning, these beliefs become ingrained in the subconscious, operating largely outside conscious awareness.

From a young age, individuals absorb messages from their environment, internalizing cultural norms, familial expectations, and societal values. These beliefs, whether empowering or limiting, shape the lens through which individuals interpret their experiences and construct their identities.

Belief systems stored in the subconscious can be diverse, encompassing notions about self-worth, competence, and one's place within the social fabric. Positive beliefs may foster confidence, resilience, and a sense of purpose, while negative or limiting beliefs can give rise to self-doubt, fear, and feelings of inadequacy. For instance, a person raised in an environment that emphasizes achievement might develop a subconscious belief that their value is contingent on success, potentially leading to anxiety and perfectionism.

Moreover, these belief systems extend beyond the realm of self-perception to influence how individuals interpret the world. Attitudes towards relationships, success, failure, and adversity are often filtered through the lens of these subconscious beliefs. For example, someone harboring a deep-seated belief in their unworthiness might approach relationships with skepticism or struggle to embrace opportunities for personal and professional growth.

Emotional Patterns

The subconscious blueprint's storage of emotional memories is a complex yet fascinating process rooted in the intricate workings of the human brain. When individuals experience emotions, particularly those laden with intensity or significance, the brain engages in the encoding of associated information. This encoding entails the storage of sensory details, thoughts, and the emotional tone of the experience, with a notable role played by the limbic system, especially the amygdala.

One key aspect of this storage involves the association of emotional memories with sensory cues. The brain tends to link emotions to various stimuli, such as sights, sounds, smells, and physical sensations. For instance, the fragrance of a particular perfume, the melody of a specific song, or the ambiance of a particular setting can serve as triggers that activate memories of past emotional experiences. These sensory cues act as pathways to access the emotional memories stored in the subconscious, often bringing forth a flood of associated feelings.

Importantly, emotional memories are frequently part of implicit memory, a non-conscious and automatic form of memory. Unlike explicit memory, which involves intentional recall, implicit memory operates beneath the surface of conscious awareness.

Consequently, the emotional memories housed in the subconscious blueprint have the potential to significantly influence an individual's behavior, reactions, and decision-making without them actively and consciously retrieving the memories. This intricate interplay between emotions, sensory cues, and subconscious processing underscores the profound impact of past experiences on our present emotional responses and behavioral patterns.

Interpersonal Dynamics

The subconscious blueprint exerts a profound influence on the templates individuals use for relationships, shaping the patterns and dynamics that characterize their connections with others. Early experiences, especially within familial and caregiving relationships, contribute significantly to the formation of attachment styles and interpersonal expectations.

These templates, deeply embedded in the subconscious, guide individuals in selecting, interacting with, and responding to romantic partners, friends, and colleagues. Whether fostering secure and trusting bonds or triggering patterns of insecurity and avoidance, the subconscious blueprint influences communication styles, emotional responses, and the degree of vulnerability one is comfortable expressing.

Impact on Decision-Making

The subconscious blueprint serves as an influential filter shaping the way individuals process information and make decisions, playing a pivotal role in their cognitive processes. Rooted in early life experiences, cultural conditioning, and learned responses, this mental filter operates behind the scenes, affecting the interpretation of incoming data.

As individuals encounter new information, the subconscious filter swiftly categorizes it based on pre-existing beliefs, biases, and emotional associations ingrained over time. This filtering mechanism helps streamline the vast amount of information received daily, allowing for quicker decision-making. This filtering process significantly influences how individuals perceive the world. It can reinforce existing beliefs by selectively attending to information that aligns with established patterns in the subconscious blueprint. Conversely, it may create a resistance to ideas that challenge or contradict these ingrained beliefs. The subconscious filter, in essence, acts as a lens through which individuals interpret their surroundings, shaping their worldview and affecting their responses to various stimuli.

The impact of the subconscious filter is particularly evident in decision-making. When faced with choices, individuals may find themselves drawn to options that resonate with their subconscious beliefs or, conversely, feel a sense of discomfort or resistance towards choices that deviate from these established patterns. This interplay between the conscious consideration of options and the automatic filtering processes of the subconscious blueprint underscores the complexity of decision-making.

Chapter 2

Biases

In the intricate tapestry of human cognition, biases form the threads that weave our perceptions, shaping the way we interpret and categorize information. These biases, often operating beneath the surface of conscious awareness and plays a pivotal role in how we make sense of the world around us. In this chapter, we'll delve into the nuances of biases and the intricate dance between our minds and incoming information.

Prominent types of biases that influence how we filter information and construct our worldview include:

Implicit Association: Unconscious Connections

Implicit association, a psychological phenomenon, refers to the unconscious connections our minds form between concepts or ideas based on previous experiences, cultural influences, and societal norms. These associations operate beneath conscious awareness, shaping our perceptions and influencing how we categorize information about the world around us. The implicit associations we form can be both subtle and powerful, impacting various aspects of our thoughts and behaviors.

At the core of implicit association is the idea that our brains create connections between concepts based on repeated exposure or cultural conditioning. For example, if an individual is consistently exposed to positive associations with certain groups, ideas, or objects, their mind may form unconscious links that influence subsequent thoughts and judgments. Conversely, negative associations can also develop, impacting how we perceive and categorize information.

Implicit associations often reveal themselves through implicit bias, where individuals unknowingly hold attitudes or stereotypes about certain groups or concepts. These biases can influence decision-making, interactions, and judgments without individuals being consciously aware of their impact.

These unconscious connections play a significant role in shaping societal attitudes and behaviors. Implicit associations contribute to the formation and reinforcement of stereotypes, prejudices, and cultural norms. For example, gender roles and racial stereotypes can be perpetuated through implicit associations, impacting how individuals categorize and interpret information related to gender or race.

The Implicit Association Test (IAT) is a widely used tool in psychological research to measure implicit associations by assessing the speed at which individuals associate concepts with positive or negative attributes. The results of these tests highlight the prevalence of implicit associations within individuals and across diverse populations, emphasizing the need for awareness and intervention to address any potential biases.

Confirmation Bias: Seeking Affirmation

Confirmation bias is a cognitive phenomenon that profoundly influences the way individuals process and interpret information, shaping their perceptions of the world. At its core, confirmation bias involves a predisposition to seek, interpret, and remember information that aligns with one's preexisting beliefs or values, while simultaneously dismissing or downplaying evidence that contradicts those beliefs.

This bias operates subtly and often unconsciously, creating a filter through which individuals selectively process information.

When confronted with new information, individuals tend to instinctively favor data that confirms what they already believe. This bias serves as a mental shortcut, offering a sense of validation and reassurance. It acts as a shield against cognitive dissonance, the discomfort that arises when confronted with conflicting information that challenges established beliefs.

Rather than engaging in a rigorous examination of all available evidence, individuals influenced by confirmation bias are more inclined to selectively focus on information that reinforces their existing convictions.

Confirmation bias manifests in various aspects of daily life, from personal beliefs and political ideologies to professional opinions. In the realm of social media, for instance, individuals may curate their online environments to be echo chambers that echo and amplify their existing views, inadvertently reinforcing confirmation bias. This selective exposure to information creates a self-reinforcing loop, where individuals are repeatedly exposed to content that validates their perspectives while avoiding contradictory information. Moreover, confirmation bias can influence the way individuals interpret ambiguous or neutral information. They may subconsciously twist or reinterpret facts to fit their existing worldview, reinforcing their initial beliefs even when faced with evidence to the contrary. This bias not only affects individual decision-making but can also contribute to the polarization of opinions within groups, as individuals seek affirmation from like-minded peers and sources.

Negativity Bias: Focusing on the Negative

Negativity bias is a cognitive phenomenon that reflects the tendency of the human mind to give more weight and attention to negative information compared to positive information. This bias influences the way individuals process, interpret, and recall information, with a heightened sensitivity to negative experiences, events, or stimuli. Rooted in evolutionary psychology, negativity bias served as an adaptive mechanism to prioritize potential threats and dangers in the ancestral environment.

In contemporary settings, negativity bias continues to shape how individuals perceive and respond to the world around them. When faced with a mix of positive and negative information, individuals tend to focus more on and be affected more strongly by the negative aspects. This bias is evident in various aspects of life, including decision-making, emotional responses, and memory recall.

In decision-making, negativity bias can lead individuals to weigh potential losses more heavily than potential gains. The fear of negative outcomes may influence choices and behaviors, even when the rational evaluation of risks and benefits suggests a more balanced perspective. This bias can impact financial decisions, risk assessments, and other areas where the avoidance of negative consequences is a primary consideration.

Emotionally, negativity bias contributes to a greater emotional impact from negative experiences. Negative events or criticisms may linger in the mind longer than positive ones, influencing mood and overall well-being. This bias can lead to a disproportionate focus on what has gone wrong, overshadowing positive aspects of a situation and contributing to feelings of stress or anxiety.

Memory recall is another domain where negativity bias is evident. Individuals are more likely to remember negative experiences or feedback compared to positive ones. This selective memory can influence perceptions of personal history and shape future expectations. The tendency to recall negative events more vividly can contribute to a pessimistic outlook and affect overall life satisfaction.

Availability Bias: Weighing the Readily Accessible

Availability bias is a cognitive shortcut that significantly influences how individuals assess and process information, often leading to systematic errors in judgment. This bias stems from the human tendency to rely on readily available information when making decisions or forming opinions, rather than seeking out more comprehensive or accurate data. It operates on the principle that information that comes to mind easily is perceived as more important or relevant, regardless of its actual significance.

When faced with a decision or tasked with forming an opinion, individuals subconsciously give more weight to information that is easily accessible or readily retrievable from their memory. This can be influenced by factors such as recency, vividness, or personal experience. Information that is more vivid or recent tends to be more accessible in memory and, therefore, is more likely to influence one's judgment, even if it is not the most accurate or representative.

One manifestation of availability bias is evident in media consumption. News stories that are sensationalized or emotionally charged may become more accessible in individuals' minds, shaping their perceptions and influencing how they categorize information about specific events or issues. In this way, the bias can lead to a distortion of reality, as individuals prioritize information that is more emotionally impactful or attention-grabbing over a more balanced understanding of a situation.

Furthermore, availability bias can affect risk perception. If vivid and memorable instances of a particular event, such as a plane crash or a natural disaster, are readily available in memory, individuals may overestimate the likelihood of such events occurring. Conversely, less dramatic but statistically more probable events may be downplayed or overlooked due to their lower memorability.

Hindsight Bias: Rearranging the Past

Hindsight bias, often referred to as the "I-knew-it-all-along" phenomenon, is a cognitive bias that influences the way individuals perceive and interpret past events. This bias involves the inclination to see events as having been predictable or foreseeable after they have occurred, even when there was little or no objective basis for predicting the outcome at the time. Hindsight bias shapes the reconstruction of the past, leading individuals to believe that they knew the outcome all along, thereby distorting their understanding of the decision-making process.

One way hindsight bias operates is through memory reconstruction. After an event has unfolded, individuals may unconsciously adjust their recollections to align with the actual outcome, reinforcing the belief that the result was more predictable than it was. This bias can lead to a sense of overconfidence and an underestimation of the uncertainty and complexity that existed before the event occurred.

Hindsight bias is often fueled by the human tendency to seek coherence and meaning in retrospect. The brain strives to create a narrative that makes sense of the past, emphasizing elements that align with the actual outcome while downplaying or omitting information that might have suggested a different outcome. This distortion of memory can impact individuals' assessments of their own decision-making abilities and those of others.

In professional and academic contexts, hindsight bias can influence how individuals evaluate the decisions of others. When looking back on historical events, individuals might mistakenly assume that the outcome was inevitable, overlooking the challenges and uncertainties that decision-makers faced at the time. This bias can affect assessments of responsibility, accountability, and the perceived competence of decision-makers.

Stereotyping: Oversimplifying Complexity

Stereotyping is a cognitive shortcut that involves oversimplifying the complexity of individuals or groups by categorizing them based on generalized characteristics. This mental process is driven by the human brain's inclination to simplify information to make sense of the world efficiently. Stereotypes, however, often result in biased and oversimplified perceptions that fail to capture the diversity and nuances inherent in individuals or groups.

When individuals encounter information about a particular social or demographic group, the brain may unconsciously rely on pre-existing stereotypes to quickly categorize and process that information. For instance, stereotypes about gender, race, ethnicity, or professions may lead individuals to make assumptions about the abilities, behaviors, or traits of individuals belonging to these groups. This oversimplification can contribute to a distorted and incomplete understanding of the complexities inherent in human behavior and identity.

Stereotyping tends to overlook individual variations within a group and perpetuates a one-size-fits-all approach to understanding people. This simplification often results in unfair judgments, reinforcing biases, and limiting our ability to appreciate the rich diversity of human experiences. For example, assuming that all members of a certain nationality share specific characteristics neglects the unique personalities, perspectives, and backgrounds that exist within that group.

The media, popular culture, and societal norms often play a role in reinforcing stereotypes. When individuals are consistently exposed to particular portrayals of certain groups in the media or societal narratives, these portrayals can become ingrained in their subconscious, shaping their perceptions and contributing to the perpetuation of stereotypes. This oversimplification can have real-world consequences, influencing social interactions, decision-making processes, and even policy formulation.

In-Group Bias: Favoring the Familiar

In-group bias, or the tendency to favor individuals or groups to which we belong, is a cognitive phenomenon that shapes the way we perceive and interact with the world. Rooted in a fundamental aspect of human social psychology, this bias is a product of our evolutionary history, where forming alliances and cooperating with those within our social circles conferred survival advantages. In contemporary society, however, in-group bias manifests as a predisposition to favor the familiar and identify more positively with individuals who share similarities with us.

When individuals identify with a particular group—whether based on shared interests, ethnicity, nationality, or other affiliations—there is a natural inclination to perceive members of that group more positively than those outside of it. This bias can lead to the formation of a mental divide between "us" and "them," influencing how we categorize, interpret, and relate to information about different social groups.

In-group bias affects various aspects of our lives, including interpersonal relationships, decision-making processes, and social dynamics. In social interactions, individuals may demonstrate a preference for members of their in-group, showing greater empathy, trust, and cooperation. This bias can also impact decision-making, as individuals may be more inclined to support policies or ideas endorsed by their in-group, even if they objectively evaluate those ideas differently in the absence of group affiliation.

Moreover, in-group bias plays a role in the formation and reinforcement of stereotypes and prejudices. The favoritism toward one's in-group can lead to negative perceptions of out-group members, contributing to social divisions and, in some cases, discrimination. This bias can be particularly pronounced in situations of competition or perceived scarcity, where individuals may intensify their in-group identification as a means of preserving resources or maintaining a sense of belonging.

Cultural Bias: Shaping Perspectives

Cultural bias plays a significant role in shaping perspectives, influencing the way individuals interpret, process, and categorize information based on their cultural background. Our cultural upbringing, encompassing traditions, values, and societal norms, acts as a lens through which we view the world. This cognitive bias impacts various aspects of cognition, affecting perceptions, attitudes, and decision-making processes.

Cultural bias operates at both conscious and unconscious levels, subtly influencing individuals' judgments and interpretations.

From communication styles and social etiquette to moral values and attitudes towards authority, cultural bias molds the mental frameworks through which we filter information. This bias can lead to the unintentional prioritization of certain perspectives or the misinterpretation of behaviors from other cultures.

One way cultural bias manifests is through ethnocentrism, where individuals evaluate other cultures based on the standards and values of their own. This can lead to the perception that one's own cultural practices are superior, potentially resulting in misunderstandings, stereotyping, and a limited appreciation for cultural diversity. Cultural bias can also impact perceptions of time, individualism vs. collectivism, and the importance placed on various aspects of life, influencing how individuals prioritize and categorize information.

Media and education systems are powerful influencers that can perpetuate or challenge cultural biases. Representations of cultures in media, literature, and educational materials may reinforce stereotypes or contribute to a more nuanced understanding of diverse perspectives. Recognizing the existence of cultural bias is crucial for creating an inclusive and respectful environment that acknowledges the richness of global diversity.

Chapter 3

The Roots of Your Patterns

Our lives are woven with the threads of experiences, both positive and negative. Within this intricate weave, behavioral patterns emerge, often influenced by the roots embedded in our past.

The roots of your patterns refer to the underlying origins or sources of the repetitive behaviors, thoughts, and habits that shape your actions, reactions, and decisions. These roots often extend into various aspects of your life, including your upbringing, experiences, cultural influences, and personal beliefs.

Understanding the roots of your patterns is essential for gaining insight into why you behave and think the way you do, and it serves as a foundation for personal growth and change. Here are some key elements that contribute to the roots of your patterns:

1 **Upbringing and Childhood Experiences:** The early years of your life, including your family environment, parenting style, and childhood experiences, significantly influence the development of behavioral and thought patterns. Positive or negative experiences during this time can leave lasting impressions.

2 **Cultural and Social Influences:** The cultural and social context in which you

grow up shapes your values, beliefs, and norms. The societal expectations, traditions, and cultural norms you are exposed to contribute to the formation of patterns in your behavior and thinking.

3 **Educational Background:** Your experiences in the educational system, including teaching styles, peer interactions, and academic achievements or challenges, can contribute to the development of certain patterns in your learning, problem-solving, and interpersonal skills.

4 **Early Role Models:** Role models, whether family members, teachers, or community figures, can play a significant role in shaping your patterns. In addition,

behaviors and attitudes observed in influential individuals during your formative years can leave a lasting impact.

5 **Traumatic Experiences:** Traumatic events or challenging experiences can create patterns as coping mechanisms. These patterns may manifest as defense mechanisms, avoidance behaviors, or specific thought patterns aimed at protecting oneself from perceived threats.

6 **Core Beliefs and Values:** Your core beliefs and values, often internalized from various sources, contribute to the formation of patterns. These beliefs influence how you perceive the world,

make decisions, and interact with others.

7 **Reinforcement and Conditioning:** Patterns can be reinforced through positive or negative feedback. If certain behaviors or thoughts lead to favorable outcomes, they are more likely to be repeated. Similarly, negative reinforcement or punishment can contribute to the avoidance of certain patterns.

8 **Media and Influences from External Sources:** The media, including television, movies, and online content, can shape your perceptions and contribute to the formation of patterns. External influences such as peer pressure and societal expectations also play a role in shaping

behavioral and thought patterns.

9 **Personal Experiences and Milestones:** Life experiences, achievements, and milestones contribute to the development of patterns. Successes and failures can shape your self-perception and influence the way you approach challenges and opportunities.

10 **Coping Mechanisms:** The strategies you adopt to cope with stress, challenges, or emotional experiences can become ingrained patterns. These coping mechanisms may be adaptive or maladaptive, influencing how you navigate various aspects of life.

Recognizing the Impact of Past Experiences

Recognizing the Impact of Past Experiences refers to the process of acknowledging and understanding how previous life events, interactions, and circumstances have shaped an individual's present beliefs, behaviors, and overall worldview. This recognition encompasses an exploration of both positive and negative experiences, recognizing the lessons learned, as well as the potential challenges and patterns that may have been established.

Through this awareness, individuals can gain insights into the root causes of certain behaviors, patterns, or emotional reactions, empowering them to make informed choices, foster personal growth, and navigate their lives more consciously. Here's a discussion on why and how recognizing the impact of past experiences is important:

1 **Understanding Current Behavior:** Past experiences serve as a blueprint for present behavior. Recognizing the impact of these experiences allows individuals to understand the origins of their habits, reactions, and decision-making processes. It provides insights into why certain patterns exist and helps individuals make more informed choices in the present.

2 **Identifying Patterns and Triggers:** Past experiences often contribute to the

formation of patterns and triggers. By reflecting on and recognizing the impact of these experiences, individuals can identify recurring themes in their lives. Understanding what triggers certain emotions or behaviors enables them to navigate challenges more effectively.

3 **Promoting Self-Compassion:** Recognizing the impact of past experiences fosters self-compassion. It allows individuals to acknowledge and validate their emotions and responses as understandable reactions to their unique life journey. This self-compassion forms a foundation for healing and personal acceptance.

4 **Healing from Trauma:** Traumatic experiences can have a lasting impact on mental and emotional well-being. Acknowledging and understanding the impact of past traumas is a crucial step in the healing process. It opens the door to seeking appropriate support, such as therapy, and implementing coping strategies to address the lingering effects of trauma.

5 **Breaking Unhealthy Patterns:** Many individuals find themselves stuck in unhealthy patterns that originated from past experiences. Recognizing these patterns is the first step toward breaking free from destructive habits and making positive changes. It empowers individuals

to choose alternative ways of thinking and behaving.

6 **Improving Interpersonal Relationships:** Understanding the impact of past experiences helps in developing healthier interpersonal dynamics. It allows individuals to communicate more effectively, set boundaries, and cultivate meaningful connections based on mutual understanding.

7 **Enhancing Emotional Intelligence:** Emotional intelligence involves recognizing and understanding one's own emotions and those of others. Reflecting on past experiences contributes to emotional intelligence by providing a foundation for understanding

the roots of various emotions. This awareness supports better emotional regulation and empathy.

8 **Facilitating Personal Growth:** Personal growth is often rooted in self-awareness, and recognizing the impact of past experiences is a key component of this process. It enables individuals to learn from their history, embrace change, and strive for continuous improvement in various aspects of their lives.

9 **Informing Decision-Making:** Past experiences shape the lenses through which individuals perceive the world. Recognizing this impact is essential for informed decision-making. It allows individuals to consider their biases,

preferences, and fears, thereby making decisions that align with their current goals and values.

10   **Creating a Foundation for Change:** Whether individuals seek to overcome challenges, develop new habits, or pursue different life paths, recognizing the impact of past experiences is foundational to creating meaningful and lasting change. It provides the clarity needed to set realistic goals and navigate the journey toward personal transformation.

Chapter 4

The Mirror Within

"The Mirror Within" is a metaphorical expression that refers to the introspective and self-reflective process of looking inward to gain insight into one's thoughts, emotions, behaviors, and overall self. It symbolizes the inner journey of self-discovery, self-awareness, and understanding.

When individuals engage in introspection, they are metaphorically holding up a mirror to examine their internal landscapes, motivations, values, strengths, weaknesses, and patterns of thinking or behaving. This concept emphasizes the importance of self-reflection as a tool for personal growth, emotional intelligence, and fostering a deeper connection with oneself.

By exploring the mirror within, individuals can gain a clearer understanding of their identity, aspirations, and areas for improvement, leading to positive and intentional life changes.

In this chapter, we'll explore the transformative power of confronting self-reflection as a catalyst for change, emphasizing the importance of embracing the discomfort that comes with honest self-examination.

Confronting Self-Reflection as a Catalyst for Change

Confronting self-reflection is a deliberate and introspective process where individuals engage in a deep examination of their thoughts, emotions, beliefs, and behaviors. It involves facing oneself with honesty, openness, and a willingness to explore one's inner landscape. Here's a closer look at the key aspects of confronting self-reflection:

1 **Introspection and Examination:** Confronting self-reflection begins with a commitment to introspection. Individuals take the time to examine their thoughts, feelings, and actions, seeking a deeper understanding of their internal world.

This introspective process is often facilitated through practices like meditation, journaling, or deep contemplation.

2 **Honesty and Openness:** Successful self-reflection requires honesty and openness. Individuals confront their own truths, acknowledging both strengths and weaknesses without judgment. This level of candor allows for a genuine exploration of personal experiences and perceptions.

3 **Questioning Assumptions and Beliefs:** Confronting self-reflection involves questioning assumptions and challenging deeply held beliefs. Individuals explore whether these beliefs align with their

current values and goals, paving the way for personal growth and transformation.

4 **Exploration of Emotional Responses:** Emotions serve as valuable indicators of underlying thoughts and experiences. Confronting self-reflection involves a careful exploration of emotional responses to various situations. Understanding the roots of these emotions helps individuals gain insight into their motivations and triggers.

5 **Recognition of Patterns:** Patterns of behavior, thought, and reaction often become apparent through self-reflection. By recognizing these patterns, individuals can understand how certain habits and tendencies have developed. This

awareness is a crucial step in initiating positive change.

6 **Goal Setting and Alignment:** Confronting self-reflection includes setting goals and aligning them with one's values. Individuals clarify their aspirations, ensuring that their objectives are authentic and meaningful. This alignment provides a clear direction for personal development.

7 **Accountability and Responsibility:** A critical aspect of self-reflection is taking accountability for one's life. Individuals confront their roles in shaping their circumstances, acknowledging responsibility for choices made. This accountability serves as a foundation for

intentional change.

8 **Embracing Growth and Adaptability:** Confronting self-reflection fosters a mindset of continuous growth and adaptability. Individuals become more open to learning from experiences, embracing change, and seeking opportunities for personal and professional development.

9 **Building Resilience:** The self-awareness gained through self-reflection contributes to emotional resilience. Understanding one's strengths and areas for improvement allows individuals to navigate challenges with greater adaptability and bounce back from setbacks.

Embracing the Discomfort of Honest Self-Examination

Embracing the discomfort of honest self-examination is a courageous and transformative process that involves confronting one's own truths, vulnerabilities, and areas for growth. This introspective journey can be challenging, but the discomfort is an integral part of personal development. Here's why and how embracing this discomfort is crucial for honest self-examination:

1 **Breaking Comfort Zones:** Honest self-examination often requires breaking out of comfort zones. Embracing discomfort means acknowledging that growth and self-discovery lie beyond the familiar and

the routine. It involves a willingness to explore aspects of oneself that may be challenging or unfamiliar.

2 **Facing Uncomfortable Truths:** Self-examination involves confronting both positive and negative aspects of oneself. Embracing discomfort means facing uncomfortable truths, such as recognizing personal shortcomings, mistakes, or areas that require improvement. This honesty is essential for meaningful self-discovery.

3 **Promoting Authenticity:** Embracing discomfort encourages individuals to be authentic and genuine in their self-examination. It involves peeling back layers of social masks and pretenses to

reveal the true self. This authenticity is a foundation for building genuine connections and understanding one's core identity.

4 **Cultivating Humility:** Honest self-examination requires humility—the ability to acknowledge imperfections and areas of growth. Embracing discomfort in this process helps individuals let go of ego and adopt a humble mindset, fostering a receptive attitude towards personal development.

5 **Encouraging Vulnerability:** Vulnerability is an inherent part of honest self-examination. Embracing discomfort means being open to vulnerability—acknowledging one's fears, insecurities,

and uncertainties. This openness allows for a deeper understanding of oneself and fosters connections with others.

6 **Overcoming Fear of Judgment:** Fear of judgment, whether from oneself or others, can create discomfort during self-examination. Embracing this discomfort involves overcoming the fear of being judged for one's thoughts, emotions, or past actions. It allows for a more objective and compassionate assessment.

7 **Fostering Resilience:** Embracing discomfort during self-examination contributes to the development of emotional resilience. The ability to navigate uncomfortable feelings and thoughts with resilience is a valuable skill

that supports overall well-being and personal growth.

8 **Initiating Positive Change:** Real change often arises from acknowledging and addressing discomfort. Embracing the discomfort of self-examination is the catalyst for positive change. It propels individuals to take intentional actions, make informed decisions, and adopt healthier habits.

9 **Enhancing Emotional Intelligence:** Honest self-examination requires a high level of emotional intelligence. Embracing discomfort allows individuals to explore the depth of their emotional responses, understand the roots of their reactions, and develop better emotional regulation

skills.

10   **Cultivating a Growth Mindset:** Individuals with a growth mindset view challenges and discomfort as opportunities for learning and development. Embracing the discomfort of self-examination aligns with a growth mindset, fostering a proactive approach to personal growth and continuous improvement.

Chapter 5

Healing Wounds from the Past

The past, with its myriad experiences, leaves an indelible mark on our emotional landscape. Healing wounds from the past refers to the process of addressing and resolving emotional, psychological, or relational traumas that have occurred in one's past. These wounds can result from a variety of experiences, such as childhood trauma, relationship conflicts, loss, or other challenging life events.

Healing involves actively working to understand, process, and integrate these past experiences, allowing individuals to move forward with a greater sense of emotional well-being and resilience. It is a transformative journey toward releasing the emotional burdens associated with past wounds and fostering personal growth and recovery.

In this chapter, we'll explore effective strategies for emotional healing and provides insights into navigating through past traumas to foster personal growth and well-being.

Strategies for Emotional Healing

Emotional healing is a multifaceted process that involves acknowledging and addressing emotional pain, trauma, or distress. Different strategies work for different individuals, and it's important to explore and find what resonates best with one's unique needs and experiences. Here are several strategies that can contribute to emotional healing:

1 **Self-Reflection and Awareness:** Begin by acknowledging and understanding your emotions. Reflect on the root causes of your emotional pain and gain insight into the patterns and triggers that contribute to it. Here are practical steps to carry out self-reflection and awareness for emotional healing:

- **Create a Safe Space:** Begin by finding a quiet and comfortable space where you can be alone with your thoughts. Minimize distractions and ensure you won't be interrupted during your reflection time.

- **Set Intentions:** Clarify your intentions for self-reflection. Whether it's understanding a specific emotional challenge, finding peace, or fostering personal growth, having a clear purpose can guide your reflection.

- **Journaling:** Express your thoughts and feelings through journaling. Write freely without judgment, allowing your emotions to flow onto the paper. This process helps externalize internal struggles and provides clarity.

- **Review Past Experiences:** Explore significant past experiences that may have contributed to current emotional challenges. Reflect on how those experiences shaped your beliefs, behaviors, and emotional responses. Acknowledge any unresolved emotions associated with these experiences.

- **Identify Patterns:** Look for recurring patterns in your emotions, reactions, and thought processes. Recognize triggers that intensify certain emotions and identify automatic responses. Understanding these patterns is essential for breaking negative cycles.

- **Practice Compassion:** Cultivate self-compassion by treating yourself with kindness and understanding. Acknowledge that everyone has flaws and makes mistakes. Be gentle with yourself as you navigate through past experiences and emotions.

2 **Therapy and Counseling:** Seek the assistance of a mental health professional. Therapists can provide a safe space for you to express your feelings, explore underlying issues, and develop coping strategies. Different therapeutic modalities, such as cognitive-behavioral therapy (CBT) or mindfulness-based approaches, may be beneficial.

3 **Mindfulness and Meditation:** Cultivate mindfulness through meditation or other mindfulness practices. These techniques can help you stay present, reduce anxiety, and promote emotional balance

by fostering awareness of your thoughts and feelings without judgment.

4 **Expressive Arts Therapy:** Engage in creative outlets such as art, music, or writing to express and process emotions. Creative expression can provide a non-verbal means of communication and release.

5 **Physical Activity:** Regular exercise has been shown to have positive effects on mood and mental well-being. Physical activity can release endorphins, reduce stress hormones, and promote a sense of accomplishment and empowerment.

6 **Connect with Supportive Relationships:** Share your feelings with trusted friends, family members, or support groups.

Connection and social support play a crucial role in emotional healing, providing validation, empathy, and a sense of belonging.

7 **Set Boundaries:** Learn to set healthy boundaries in relationships and situations that may be contributing to emotional distress. Establishing and maintaining boundaries is crucial for self-care and protecting your emotional well-being.

8 **Gratitude Practices:** Cultivate gratitude by focusing on positive aspects of your life. Gratitude practices, such as keeping a gratitude journal, can shift your perspective and foster a more positive mindset.

9 **Holistic Approaches:** Explore holistic approaches like acupuncture, yoga, or aromatherapy. These practices may complement traditional therapeutic methods and contribute to overall emotional well-being.

10 **Seeking Closure:** When possible, seek closure from past traumas or unresolved issues. This may involve forgiveness, acceptance, or finding meaning in challenging experiences.

Navigating Through Past Traumas

Navigating through past traumas is a profound and often challenging journey that requires intentional effort and self-compassion. Trauma can have lasting effects on mental, emotional, and physical well-being, but there are strategies to help individuals heal and reclaim a sense of agency over their lives:

Acknowledge and Validate

Acknowledging the existence of past traumas and validating the associated emotions is a courageous and transformative process that forms the bedrock of emotional healing. It begins with a profound acknowledgment of the reality of the traumatic experiences one has endured.

This acknowledgment entails facing the often painful and uncomfortable truths of the past, recognizing that these events have left indelible imprints on one's psyche. Whether the traumas are large or small, their significance lies in their impact on the individual, and validating this impact is the first step toward reclaiming agency over one's emotional well-being.

Validating the associated emotions is an equally vital component of this healing journey. It involves embracing a compassionate and non-judgmental stance toward the range of emotions that surface as a result of past traumas.

Whether it be profound sadness, intense anger, paralyzing fear, or a complex amalgamation of feelings, acknowledging that these emotions are legitimate responses is key.

Each emotion serves as a valid expression of the individual's internal experience, a testament to the challenges faced and the resilience demonstrated in the aftermath of trauma.

This process of acknowledgment and validation is essential for several reasons. Firstly, it facilitates a deep understanding of the emotional landscape, allowing individuals to connect with their inner selves and unravel the intricacies of their emotional responses.

Secondly, it establishes a foundation of self-compassion. By acknowledging the existence of past traumas and validating associated emotions, individuals grant themselves permission to feel without judgment, fostering a sense of kindness and understanding toward their own experiences.

Moreover, acknowledging and validating past traumas opens the door to healing. It creates a space where individuals can begin to release the emotional burden carried from the past, making room for growth and resilience.

Ultimately, this acknowledgment and validation pave the way for a more profound and authentic healing journey, allowing individuals to reclaim agency over their narrative and move forward with resilience and self-compassion.

Professional Support

Mental health professionals play a pivotal role in trauma recovery, offering specialized guidance and support to individuals navigating the complex aftermath of traumatic experiences. One primary aspect of their role is providing a safe and confidential space where individuals can openly share their experiences without fear of judgment. This therapeutic alliance is fundamental in establishing trust, a crucial foundation for effective trauma recovery.

Another crucial role mental health professionals fulfill is the assessment and diagnosis of trauma-related conditions. They possess the expertise to identify symptoms of trauma-related disorders such as PTSD (Post-Traumatic Stress Disorder), anxiety, and depression. Through thorough evaluation, mental health professionals can tailor their approach to meet the unique needs of each individual, recognizing that trauma manifests differently for each person.

In the therapeutic process, mental health professionals employ evidence-based interventions to help individuals process and make sense of their traumatic experiences. Techniques such as Cognitive Behavioral Therapy (CBT), Eye Movement Desensitization and Reprocessing (EMDR), and other trauma-focused modalities are employed to address symptoms, reframe negative thought patterns, and facilitate emotional healing. These interventions are carefully selected based on the individual's specific symptoms and needs.

Importantly, mental health professionals

act as educators, providing individuals with information about the effects of trauma on the mind and body. Understanding the neurobiological and psychological aspects of trauma empowers individuals to comprehend their reactions and emotions, reducing feelings of shame or self-blame. Psychoeducation helps normalize the range of responses to trauma, fostering self-compassion and resilience.

In addition to therapeutic interventions, mental health professionals often collaborate with individuals to develop coping mechanisms and self-care strategies. These tools empower individuals to manage distressing symptoms, regulate emotions, and build resilience in the face of ongoing challenges. The goal is to equip individuals with practical skills that enhance their ability to navigate the complexities of trauma recovery both during and between therapy sessions.

Moreover, mental health professionals may play a crucial role in coordinating care and advocating for their clients within the broader healthcare system. They can collaborate with other healthcare providers, ensuring a comprehensive approach to trauma recovery that addresses both mental and physical health needs. Advocacy may involve liaising with support networks, employers, or legal entities to create an environment conducive to healing.

Create a Safe Space

Creating a safe space for trauma healing is a thoughtful and intentional process that involves both physical and emotional considerations. Begin by choosing a physical environment that makes you feel secure and at ease. This could be a room in your home, a cozy corner with soft lighting, or any place where you can have privacy. Arrange the space with comforting items, such as blankets, pillows, or meaningful objects that bring a sense of calm.

Establish a routine for your healing space. Set aside dedicated time each day or week for self-reflection, meditation, or therapeutic activities. Consistency is key, as it helps signal to your mind that this is a designated time for healing. Consider incorporating elements like soothing music, aromatherapy, or gentle lighting to enhance the calming atmosphere.

In addition to the physical environment, focus on the emotional safety of your healing space. Create boundaries that protect your emotional well-being and ensure that you won't be interrupted or disturbed during your healing time. Communicate these boundaries to those around you, so they understand the importance of respecting your space.

Integrate activities that promote self-expression and self-discovery. Journaling, art, or other creative outlets can be powerful tools for processing and understanding your emotions. Allow yourself the freedom to explore your feelings without judgment, and embrace the healing journey as a process rather than a destination.

Consider seeking professional support. Whether through therapy, counseling, or support groups, having a trained professional guide you through your healing journey can provide valuable insights and coping strategies. Your safe space can be a place to reflect on and implement what you learn in therapy.

Finally, practice self-compassion. Healing from trauma is a gradual process, and it's important to acknowledge your progress and be patient with yourself. Celebrate small victories and be gentle in moments of difficulty. Your safe space should be a refuge where you can cultivate self-love and resilience as you navigate the path toward healing.

Self-Compassion and Patience

In the intricate landscape of trauma healing, self-compassion stands as a guiding light, offering individuals a crucial balm for the emotional wounds left in the wake of traumatic experiences. The role of self-compassion lies in fostering a tender relationship with oneself, one that refrains from self-blame and judgment.

When confronted with the aftermath of trauma, individuals who cultivate self-compassion grant themselves the grace to acknowledge their pain without the weight of unwarranted guilt. This compassionate approach becomes a salient force in creating an internal environment where vulnerabilities can be explored openly and healing can take root.

By extending the same kindness to oneself that one might offer a friend, self-compassion lays the foundation for a transformative and nurturing healing journey.

Complementing self-compassion is the indispensable virtue of patience. The trajectory of trauma healing rarely adheres to a linear path; it is marked by peaks and valleys, progress and setbacks. Patience becomes a steadying force, urging individuals to navigate this complex terrain with a tempered expectation of gradual growth.

Recognizing that healing is an ongoing, non-linear process, patience invites individuals to embrace each step forward, no matter how small, and to weather the moments of frustration or impatience that may arise.

The interplay between self-compassion and patience is profound, creating a symbiotic relationship that fortifies individuals on their healing journey. When faced with the inevitable challenges of trauma recovery, self-compassion becomes the wellspring of emotional sustenance. It enables individuals to respond to setbacks or moments of difficulty with understanding rather than self-condemnation.

Patience, in turn, supports a mindset that views the healing process as an evolving journey, not a destination. Together, they create a resilient framework, empowering individuals to confront the complexities of trauma recovery with self-worth and the endurance needed for lasting transformation.

Gradual Exposure

Gradual exposure to traumatic memories serves as a therapeutic cornerstone in the intricate process of trauma healing. This evidence-based approach recognizes that confronting distressing memories in a controlled and systematic manner can be instrumental in diminishing their emotional impact.

The method involves a structured and gradual approach to revisiting the traumatic experiences, allowing individuals to face and process their emotions incrementally. This intentional exposure is designed to empower individuals to gain a sense of mastery over their emotional responses, contributing to the overarching goal of healing.

One of the primary roles of gradual exposure is to empower emotional processing. Traumatic memories are often laden with intense and overwhelming emotions that can be challenging to navigate. By systematically exposing individuals to these memories in a therapeutic context, the approach encourages a careful examination of associated emotions.

This intentional engagement facilitates the untangling of complex emotional responses, providing individuals with the opportunity to confront, understand, and ultimately process their emotions in a supportive and guided environment.

Moreover, gradual exposure plays a pivotal role in reframing negative associations linked to traumatic memories. Individuals often develop maladaptive beliefs and associations related to their traumatic experiences. The controlled and gradual nature of exposure therapy allows for a deliberate dismantling of these negative associations.

As individuals revisit the memories in a safe and therapeutic setting, they can work towards creating new, more adaptive perspectives. Over time, this process contributes to reshaping the narrative surrounding the traumatic events, fostering a sense of empowerment and control.

The effectiveness of gradual exposure lies in its ability to promote emotional regulation. By confronting traumatic memories gradually, individuals develop skills to manage and regulate their emotional responses.

This regulated exposure aids in preventing overwhelming emotional distress, allowing individuals to engage with their traumatic experiences in a way that promotes healing rather than retraumatization. The process encourages the development of coping mechanisms, enhancing emotional resilience in the face of distressing memories.

Mindfulness and Grounding Techniques

Incorporate mindfulness and grounding techniques into daily life. Techniques such as deep breathing, meditation, or focusing on sensory experiences can help manage overwhelming emotions and keep individuals grounded in the present moment.

Cultivate Supportive Relationships

Surround yourself with supportive and understanding individuals. Building a network of friends, family, or support groups can provide a sense of belonging and encouragement during the healing process.

Educate Yourself

Learn about trauma and its effects. Understanding the psychological and physiological aspects of trauma can empower individuals to navigate through their experiences with greater insight and self-awareness.

Physical Well-Being

Prioritize physical well-being. Regular exercise, a balanced diet, and adequate sleep contribute to overall mental health and resilience.

Set Realistic Goals

Set realistic and achievable goals for yourself. Breaking down the healing journey into smaller, manageable steps can foster a sense of accomplishment and progress.

Celebrate Progress

Celebrate the milestones and progress made along the way. Acknowledge and honor the resilience it takes to confront and overcome past traumas.

Chapter 6

Tools for Transformation

Embarking on a journey of personal transformation involves equipping oneself with the right tools to break free from negative patterns and cultivate resilience. This chapter explores practical techniques for initiating change, breaking negative patterns, and building the emotional strength needed for lasting transformation.

Practical Techniques for Breaking Negative Patterns

Breaking negative patterns requires a combination of self-awareness, commitment, and practical techniques to replace old habits with healthier alternatives. Here are some practical techniques to help break negative patterns:

1 **Self-Reflection:** Begin by identifying the negative patterns you want to change. Reflect on the triggers, emotions, and consequences associated with these patterns. Understanding the root cause is crucial for effective change. Here are some examples of triggers, emotions they generate and their consequences:

Trigger: Criticism from Others

- **Emotion:** Insecurity
- **Consequence:** Seeking constant validation, defensiveness, or withdrawal to avoid criticism.

Trigger: Failure or Rejection

- **Emotion:** Shame or Worthlessness

- **Consequence:** Avoidance of challenges, self-sabotage, or overcompensation to prove worth.

Trigger: Conflict in Relationships

- **Emotion:** Fear or Anxiety

- **Consequence:** People-pleasing behavior, avoiding confrontation, or becoming overly submissive.

Trigger: Feeling Overwhelmed

- **Emotion:** Stress or Anxiety

- **Consequence:** Procrastination, avoidance, or engaging in unhealthy coping mechanisms.

Trigger: Perceived Abandonment

- **Emotion:** Fear of Abandonment

- **Consequence:** Clinginess, excessive dependence, or pushing others away to avoid potential rejection.

Trigger: Unmet Expectations

- **Emotion:** Frustration or Disappointment

- **Consequence:** Negative self-talk, resentment, or withdrawing from future opportunities.

Trigger: Feeling Unappreciated

- **Emotion:** Neglect or Unworthiness

- **Consequence:** Seeking validation through external means, resentment, or withdrawing from relationships.

Trigger: Uncertainty or Change

- **Emotion:** Anxiety or Fear of the Unknown

- **Consequence:** Resistance to change, rigidity, or excessive planning as a coping mechanism.

Trigger: Comparisons to Others

- **Emotion:** Inadequacy or Envy
- **Consequence:** Overworking, imitating others, or withdrawing due to a fear of not measuring up.

Trigger: Feeling Helpless

- **Emotion:** Powerlessness
- **Consequence:** Victim mentality, passivity, or avoiding taking responsibility.

2 **Set Clear Goals:** Define specific and realistic goals for breaking negative patterns. Clearly outline what you want to achieve and set measurable milestones

to track your progress.

3 **Create Awareness:** Develop mindfulness and self-awareness to recognize when negative patterns are about to emerge. Pay attention to your thoughts, emotions, and behaviors in different situations.

4 **Interrupt the Pattern:** Actively interrupt negative patterns when you notice them. This could involve taking a pause, deep breaths, or engaging in a brief physical activity to disrupt the automatic response.

5 **Replace with Positive Habits:** Identify positive behaviors or habits that can replace the negative ones. Intentionally practice these alternatives until they

become more ingrained. For example, if negative patterns involve negative self-talk, replace it with positive affirmations. Consistently reinforce these positive affirmations whenever the negative patterns resurface, allowing the repetition to counteract and eventually replace the harmful thought patterns.

6 **Implement Behavioral Changes Gradually:** Instead of trying to change everything at once, focus on one aspect of the negative pattern at a time. Gradual changes are more sustainable and less overwhelming.

7 **Utilize Cognitive-Behavioral Techniques:** Cognitive-Behavioral Therapy (CBT) techniques can be effective in challenging

and changing negative thought patterns. This may involve questioning irrational beliefs, reframing negative thoughts, and developing more constructive perspectives.

8 **Seek Support:** Share your goals with friends, family, or a therapist. Having a support system can provide encouragement, accountability, and valuable insights.

9 **Develop Coping Strategies:** Identify healthy coping strategies for dealing with stress, anxiety, or other triggers that contribute to negative patterns. This might include practicing mindfulness, exercise, or engaging in activities you enjoy.

10   **Journaling:** Keep a journal to track your thoughts, emotions, and behaviors. This can help you identify patterns, triggers, and progress over time. Reflecting on your journal entries provides insights into your journey.

11 **Positive Visualization:** Visualize yourself breaking free from negative patterns and engaging in positive behaviors. This mental rehearsal can help rewire your brain and reinforce a more positive mindset.

12 **Accountability:** Share your progress with someone you trust or join a support group. Knowing that others are aware of your goals can provide an extra layer of accountability.

13**Professional Guidance:** Consider seeking the help of a therapist or counselor who specializes in behavior change. They can offer personalized strategies and support to address the underlying causes of negative patterns.

Chapter 7

Creating a Vision of Your True Self

Creating a vision of your true self involves cultivating a clear and authentic understanding of who you are at your core, independent of societal expectations, external influences, or past conditioning. It is about envisioning the most genuine, empowered, and fulfilled version of yourself. This process often involves self-reflection, introspection, and intentional goal-setting.

Let's now delve into the transformative process of designing your authentic identity and setting goals for personal growth, emphasizing the power of envisioning the person you aspire to become.

Designing Your Authentic Identity

Designing your authentic identity involves a purposeful and intentional exploration of who you truly are, free from societal expectations, external pressures, and imposed identities. It's about crafting a self-concept that aligns with your core values, beliefs, and aspirations. Here are key considerations for designing your authentic identity:

1 **Self-Reflection:** Start by engaging in deep self-reflection. Examine your values, passions, strengths, and areas of growth. Understand your motivations, desires, and the things that bring you a sense of

fulfillment.

2 **Clarify Core Values:** Identify and articulate your core values. These are the principles that guide your decisions, actions, and overall life direction. Ensuring that your identity is rooted in these values contributes to authenticity.

3 **Embrace Individuality:** Celebrate your individuality and uniqueness. Recognize that your authentic identity doesn't need to conform to societal norms or expectations. Embrace the aspects that make you distinctly you.

4 **Challenge Societal Expectations:** Question and challenge societal expectations and stereotypes that may have influenced your self-perception.

Consider how societal norms may have shaped your identity and whether they align with your true self.

5 **Define Personal Boundaries:** Clearly define and establish personal boundaries. Know what is acceptable and unacceptable in your interactions and relationships. This helps in maintaining authenticity and self-respect.

6 **Explore Your Passions:** Actively explore your interests and passions. Engaging in activities you genuinely enjoy contributes to a sense of authenticity and helps you connect with your true self.

7 **Cultivate Self-Awareness:** Cultivate self-awareness by paying attention to your thoughts, emotions, and behaviors.

Understand how you respond to various situations and consider whether those responses align with your authentic self.

8 **Express Your Truth:** Be open and honest about your thoughts, feelings, and beliefs. Authenticity involves expressing your truth, even when it may be challenging or unpopular.

9 **Learn and Grow:** Recognize that your authentic identity is a dynamic and evolving concept. Embrace opportunities for learning, growth, and self-improvement, adapting your identity as you gain new insights and experiences.

10 **Mindfulness Practices:** Engage in mindfulness practices to stay present and connected with your authentic self.

Mindfulness can help you navigate challenges, make conscious choices, and foster a deeper understanding of yourself.

11 **Celebrate Your Achievements:** Acknowledge and celebrate your achievements, no matter how small. Recognizing your accomplishments reinforces a positive self-image and encourages the authentic expression of your capabilities.

Setting Goals for Personal Growth

Setting goals for personal growth is a powerful and intentional way to enhance various aspects of your life, fostering self-improvement and fulfillment. Here's a guide on how to set effective goals for personal growth:

1 **Self-Reflection:** Begin by reflecting on your current strengths, weaknesses, values, and areas where you'd like to see improvement. Consider what aspects of your life are most meaningful to you.

2 **Define Your Values:** Identify your core values. Your goals should align with these values to ensure that your personal growth journey is authentic and meaningful.

3 **Clarify Your Vision:** Envision the person you want to become. What does personal growth look like for you? Clearly define your vision, considering different aspects of your life, such as relationships, career, health, and well-being.

4 **Set SMART Goals:** Ensure that your goals are Specific, Measurable, Achievable, Relevant, and Time-Bound (SMART). This framework provides clarity and structure, making it easier to track progress and stay motivated.

5 **Break Down Larger Goals:** If you have long-term or larger goals, break them down into smaller, manageable steps. This makes the process less overwhelming and allows you to celebrate achievements along the way.

6 **Prioritize Goals:** Prioritize your goals based on their significance and impact on your life. Focus on a few key goals at a time to avoid spreading yourself too thin.

7 **Create an Action Plan:** Develop a detailed action plan outlining the specific steps you need to take to achieve each goal. Break down the plan into daily, weekly, or monthly tasks to maintain consistent progress.

8 **Track Your Progress:** Regularly assess your progress. Tracking your achievements provides motivation and allows for adjustments to your approach if necessary. Celebrate milestones and use setbacks as learning opportunities.

9 **Stay Flexible:** Be flexible and open to adapting your goals as circumstances change. Life is dynamic, and being able to adjust your goals ensures that they remain relevant to your evolving needs

and aspirations.

10   **Seek Accountability:** Share your goals with a trusted friend, family member, or mentor. Having someone to hold you accountable can provide support, encouragement, and an external perspective on your progress.

11 **Cultivate a Growth Mindset:** Adopt a growth mindset by viewing challenges and setbacks as opportunities for learning and improvement. Embrace the belief that your abilities and intelligence can be developed through dedication and hard work.

12 **Incorporate Self-Care:** Ensure that your goals incorporate self-care practices. Personal growth is holistic, and taking

care of your mental, emotional, and physical well-being is essential for sustainable growth.

13 **Reflect and Adjust:** Regularly reflect on your goals, assessing what is and isn't working. Be willing to adjust your goals or action plan if needed. Continuous reflection enhances self-awareness and adaptability.

14 **Celebrate Achievements:** Celebrate your achievements, no matter how small. Acknowledging and celebrating your progress reinforces positive behavior and motivates you to continue working toward your personal growth goals.

Chapter 8

Navigating Change and Embracing Growth

Change is a constant companion in the journey of life, and navigating it with resilience and a growth mindset is key to personal development.

Navigating change and embracing growth involves the intentional and adaptive process of maneuvering through life's transitions, challenges, and opportunities with a positive and forward-thinking mindset. It encompasses a willingness to embrace uncertainty, learn from experiences, and cultivate personal and professional development.

In this chapter, we'll explore the transformative process of embracing change, the journey of self-discovery, and overcoming challenges along the way.

Embracing the Journey of Transformation

Embracing the journey of transformation is a profound and intentional process of personal development and growth. It involves recognizing the need for change, navigating through challenges, and evolving into a more authentic and empowered version of oneself. Here are key aspects of embracing the journey of transformation:

1 **Self-Discovery:** The journey begins with self-discovery, gaining a deeper understanding of one's values, beliefs, strengths, and areas for growth. This self-awareness forms the foundation for meaningful transformation.

2 **Clarifying Intentions:** Clearly defining the intentions and goals for transformation. Whether it's improving mental well-being, building healthier relationships, or pursuing professional growth, having a clear purpose guides the journey.

3 **Acceptance of Imperfection:** Embracing the imperfections and vulnerabilities inherent in the human experience. Recognizing that transformation is a process, and setbacks are opportunities

for learning and refinement rather than indicators of failure.

4 **Courage to Change:** Developing the courage to embrace change and step out of the comfort zone. Transformation often requires confronting fears, challenging limiting beliefs, and taking risks to move toward a more fulfilling life.

5 **Mindset Shift:** Cultivating a growth mindset that sees challenges as opportunities for learning and growth. A positive and open mindset enhances resilience and fosters a more constructive approach to transformation.

6 **Adapting to Change:** Learning to adapt to changes in circumstances, perspectives, and priorities. Being open to reevaluate

and adjust goals as needed while staying committed to the overall journey of transformation.

7 **Patience and Perseverance:** Recognizing that transformation is a gradual process that requires patience and perseverance. Real change often takes time, and setbacks are a natural part of the journey. Maintaining a resilient attitude is crucial.

8 **Seeking Support:** Building a support system of friends, family, mentors, or professionals who can offer guidance, encouragement, and accountability. Having a network to share the transformational journey enhances resilience and motivation.

9 **Learning from Setbacks:** Viewing setbacks as opportunities for reflection and learning rather than as obstacles. Analyzing challenges allows for the identification of patterns, adjustments to strategies, and continued growth.

10 **Celebrating Milestones:** Acknowledging and celebrating the small victories and milestones along the way. Recognizing progress reinforces positive behavior and provides motivation to continue the transformative journey.

11 **Expressing Gratitude:** Cultivating gratitude for the experiences, lessons, and people encountered during the journey. Gratitude fosters a positive outlook and deepens the understanding

of the transformative process.

12 **Integration of Lessons:** Integrating the lessons learned into daily life. Transformation is not just about change for its own sake but about applying newfound wisdom and insights to create a more meaningful and purposeful existence.

13 **Connecting with Purpose:** Aligning the journey of transformation with a sense of purpose and values. Connecting with a higher purpose provides a guiding compass and sustains motivation during challenging times.

14 **Embracing the Unpredictable:** Embracing the unpredictability of the transformational journey. Life is dynamic,

and transformation often involves adapting to unexpected twists and turns with resilience and a sense of curiosity.

15. **Living Authentically:** Striving to live authentically, aligning actions with true values and desires. Transformation is about becoming more genuine and true to oneself, creating a life that reflects inner authenticity.

Overcoming Challenges on the Path to Self-Discovery

Embarking on the journey of self-discovery is a deeply personal and transformative experience, but it often comes with its own set of challenges. Overcoming these challenges is an integral part of the process, as they contribute to personal growth and resilience. Here are some common obstacles on the path to self-discovery and ways to overcome them:

1 **Fear of the Unknown:**

Solution: Embrace uncertainty as an opportunity for growth. Understand that self-discovery is a continual process, and not having all the answers is part of the journey. Cultivate a mindset that sees the unknown as a space for potential rather than a source of anxiety.

2 **Social Expectations and Pressure:**

Solution: Challenge societal norms and expectations that may hinder your authentic self. Surround yourself with supportive individuals who encourage your personal growth. Focus on your values and aspirations rather than conforming to external expectations.

3 Self-Doubt and Insecurity:

Solution: Practice self-compassion and mindfulness. Acknowledge that self-discovery is a process, and it's okay not to have everything figured out. Celebrate small victories and reflect on your strengths. Seek support from friends, family, or a mentor to boost your confidence.

4 Past Trauma and Emotional Baggage:

Solution: Addressing past trauma is crucial for self-discovery. Consider seeking professional help, such as therapy, to navigate and heal from past wounds. Understand that healing is a gradual process, and it's okay to take the necessary time to work through emotional baggage.

5 **Comfort Zone Resistance:**

Solution: Challenge yourself to step outside your comfort zone. Growth often occurs when you face new experiences and overcome challenges. Set realistic goals that push your boundaries, gradually expanding your comfort zone.

6 **Comparisons with Others:**

Solution: Avoid comparing your journey to others'. Each individual's path is unique, and everyone progresses at their own pace. Focus on your personal growth and celebrate your achievements rather than measuring them against others.

7 Lack of Self-Awareness:

Solution: Cultivate self-awareness through introspection, mindfulness, and self-reflection. Regularly check in with yourself to understand your thoughts, emotions, and motivations. Journaling, meditation, and seeking feedback from trusted friends can aid in developing a deeper understanding of yourself.

8 Perfectionism:

Solution: Recognize that perfection is unattainable, and the pursuit of it can be detrimental to self-discovery. Embrace imperfections as opportunities for learning and growth. Allow yourself to make mistakes and view them as valuable lessons.

9 Impatience:

Solution: Understand that self-discovery is a lifelong journey. Patience is key, as personal growth takes time. Set realistic expectations and appreciate the small steps forward. Focus on the process rather than fixating on immediate results.

10 Lack of Direction:

Solution: Start with small steps. Explore different interests, engage in activities that bring you joy, and pay attention to what resonates with you. The more you experiment and explore, the clearer your sense of direction will become.

Chapter 9

Cultivating Lasting Change

Cultivating lasting change involves intentionally and sustainably transforming aspects of oneself, behaviors, or systems over an extended period. This process goes beyond short-term adjustments and aims to create enduring positive shifts. Whether on a personal level or within organizations, cultivating lasting change requires thoughtful planning, consistent effort, and a commitment to long-term growth.

In this chapter, we'll explore the intricacies of cultivating lasting change, emphasizing the importance of establishing habits for continued growth and sustaining the journey towards authenticity.

Establishing Habits for Continued Growth

Establishing habits for continued growth is a powerful strategy for achieving long-term personal development. By integrating positive habits into your daily routine, you create a structured and consistent approach to self-improvement. Here are key principles to consider when establishing habits for continued growth:

1 **Identify Areas for Growth:** Reflect on areas of your life where you want to see improvement. This could include personal development, career, relationships, health, or any other aspect. Identifying

specific areas for growth provides clarity and direction.

2 **Set Clear and Achievable Goals:** Break down your growth aspirations into clear, achievable goals. Make sure your goals are specific, measurable, and realistic. This helps create a roadmap for your habits and provides a sense of accomplishment as you make progress.

3 **Start Small:** Begin with manageable habits to avoid overwhelm. Starting small allows you to build momentum and increases the likelihood of success. Once these habits become ingrained, you can gradually introduce more challenging ones.

4 **Consistency is Key:** Consistency is crucial when establishing habits. Regularly practice your chosen habits, ideally incorporating them into your daily routine. Consistency reinforces the behavior and makes it more likely to become a permanent part of your lifestyle.

5 **Create a Routine:** Incorporate your growth habits into a daily or weekly routine. Having a designated time for these activities makes them easier to remember and integrate into your life. Consistency in timing can also help reinforce the habit.

6 **Build a Keystone Habit:** Identify a keystone habit, a single habit that has a positive impact on other areas of your life. For example, regular exercise often leads to improved energy levels, better sleep, and increased productivity. Focusing on a keystone habit can catalyze overall growth.

7 **Track Your Progress:** Keep track of your habits and their impact on your growth journey. This could be done through a journal, a habit-tracking app, or other means. Monitoring progress provides motivation and allows you to make adjustments as needed.

8 **Accountability:** Share your goals and habits with a friend, family member, or colleague who can provide support and hold you accountable. Having someone to share your progress and challenges with enhances your commitment to continued growth.

9 **Learn and Iterate:** Stay open to learning and adjusting your habits based on your experiences. If a particular habit is not yielding the desired results, analyze why and make necessary adjustments. The ability to adapt is essential for sustained growth.

10 **Practice Mindfulness:** Cultivate mindfulness in your daily habits. Be present and fully engaged in the activities

you're incorporating for growth. Mindfulness enhances the effectiveness of your efforts and deepens your connection to the habits you're establishing.

11 **Celebrate Milestones:** Acknowledge and celebrate your achievements along the way. Celebrating milestones, no matter how small, reinforces positive behavior and provides motivation to continue on your growth journey.

12 **Be Patient:** Recognize that growth is a gradual process. Be patient with yourself as you work towards your goals. Habits take time to form, and genuine, lasting growth is often a journey rather than a destination.

13 **Continuously Expand Your Habits:** As you achieve success with initial habits, consider adding new ones to further expand your personal development. This ongoing expansion ensures that your growth journey remains dynamic and aligned with evolving aspirations.

14 **Reflect and Refine:** Regularly reflect on your habits, their impact, and how they contribute to your growth. Refine your approach based on insights gained through reflection, ensuring that your habits remain aligned with your evolving goals.

Conclusion

As we reach the conclusion of "Infinite Reflections: Recognizing Patterns, Healing from the Past, and Creating the True You," the journey of self-discovery continues to unfold, expanding into the limitless horizon of possibilities.

In the exploration of patterns and the recognition of reflections, we have confronted the shadows of the past, woven the threads of healing, and witnessed the emergence of the authentic self.

This book is a juncture where the insights gained become the seeds for ongoing transformation. The concluding pages invite you to carry the torch of self-awareness into the uncharted territories of your future. For every realization, every revelation, is a stepping stone toward a more profound understanding of who you are and who you can become.

The journey toward the true self is a continuous process—one that requires commitment, self-compassion, and a willingness to embrace the ever-changing nature of life. As you navigate the intricate dance of patterns, remember that each step forward is an affirmation of your resilience and a testament to your capacity for growth.

The true you, uncovered and celebrated within these pages, is not a static destination but a dynamic existence in perpetual evolution. The reflections in the mirror of your being will continue to shift, revealing new facets, new possibilities. Cherish this process, for it is the essence of the human experience—the eternal journey of self-discovery.

May the wisdom gained from these pages accompany you on your ongoing quest for authenticity, healing, and fulfillment. As you step into the boundless realm of your potential, may you find solace in the knowledge that the patterns you recognize, the wounds you heal, and the true you that emerges are integral threads in the grand tapestry of existence.

"Infinite Reflections" is an invitation to a lifelong exploration—a reminder that within the depths of your being, an infinite well of wisdom, resilience, and authenticity awaits. The concluding words mark not an end but a commencement—a commencement of a new chapter in the ever-evolving story of your true self.